Raised in Birmingham, UK, Fiona studied European Studies at the University of Manchester Institute of Science and Technology.

As a chartered financial advisor, she has written articles for professional journals and press. Fiona and her husband also run a personalised poetry business; both enjoy writing. This is Fiona's second book.

She has two children, Matt, and Naomi, plus lots of animals. She loves to get inspiration from nature. Animals can teach so much with the way they live.

Fiona Whyte

If I Don't Come Back

Austin Macauley Publishers™
London • Cambridge • New York • Sharjah

A CIP catalogue record for this title is available from the British Library.

ISBN 9781035815982 (Paperback)
ISBN 9781035815999 (ePub e-book)

www.austinmacauley.com

First Published 2024
Austin Macauley Publishers Ltd®
1 Canada Square
Canary Wharf
London
E14 5AA

This book is for James and Jennifer. Be brave like your mother.

Thank you to my husband, Robin, for his continued support.

A hummingbird created a warm nest in a tall tree.

She laid three eggs in three days.
For ten days, she watched over the eggs and kept them warm.

On the tenth day, the eggs began to hatch.
She felt her heart burst with pride every time a tiny beak broke through the shell.

The hummingbird fed the tiny birds and cared for them.

she told them every day how much she loved them.

One by one, the chicks were able
to see.
They looked at the world around them, and they
longed to explore.
"In time, you will be ready to discover the world for
yourselves," she told them. "Now I need to keep
you safe."
Every day, the hummingbird left the nest to get
food for her growing babies.
She returned with insects, nectar and soft fruit
to feed the chicks.
Over three weeks, they were growing into perfect
little hummingbirds.

One day, she found a hawk's feather and brought it back to the nest.

"If I don't come back, this feather will give you my courage," she told her babies.

A day later, she found an eagle's feather and brought it back to the nest.
"If I don't come back, this feather will give you my strength," she said to the chicks.

On the third day, she found a dove's feather and brought it back to the nest.

"If I don't come back, this feather will give you my love," she reassured them.

Over the next few days, the hummingbird used the feathers to make the nest the most beautiful home in the tree.

When the nest was finished, she hugged her babies and left in search of food.
The hummingbird flew into the sky and disappeared over the horizon.
The chicks waited for the hummingbird to return and, one by one, their stomachs began to hurt with hunger.
The oldest chick began to flap its wings and flew straight up in the air. it got scared but looked at the hawk's feather in the nest and gained the courage to try again.
"We can go now and get food for ourselves," it said to the other two chicks after a few more attempts to fly.

The second chick looked at the eagle’s feather and found the strength to prepare to launch from the nest.

The third chick saw the dove's feather and felt the hummingbird's love fill its body. The chick was ready to fly.

The three little hummingbirds flew out into the world together.
Each little bird was filled with the courage of a hawk, the strength of an eagle and the love of a dove.
They carried the memory of the feathers and the spirit of their mother with them always.

Fiona Keogh ©

The End